THE
1992 CHARLTON
COIN GUIDE

31ST EDITION

Dealer's Buying Prices For
Canadian, Newfoundland and Maritime Coinage
Canadian Medals, Tokens and Paper Money
United States and World Gold Coinage

W. K. Cross
Publisher

_ ; 18501

The Charlton Press

AUG 1 6 1991

Toronto, Ontario
Birmingham, Michigan

ISSN 0706-0459
ISBN 0-88968-088-4

PRINTED IN CANADA
Editorial Office: Charlton Press
2010 Yonge Street
Toronto, Ontario
M4S 1Z9

CONTENTS

Introduction 4

Coins of Canada:

Nova Scotia 7

Prince Edward Island 7

New Brunswick 7

Newfoundland 9

Province of Canada 14

Dominion of Canada 15

Collectors Issues 32

Olympic Coins 38

Paper Money of Canada:

Province of Canada 45

Dominion of Canada 45

Bank of Canada 50

Colonial Coins and Tokens

Newfoundland 59

Prince Edward Island 60

Nova Scotia 62

New Brunswick 65

Lower Canada 66

Wellington Tokens 69

Upper Canada Tokens 70

Province of Canada 71

Anonymous and Miscellaneous 72

Canadian Medals 75

Coins of the United States 81

World Gold Coins 95

Appendix - Gold and Silver
Bullion Values 98

While every care has been taken to ensure accuracy in the compilation of the data in this guide, the publisher cannot accept responsibility for typographical errors.

INTRODUCTION

It is more difficult to obtain old coins in circulation, much more so than it was twenty years ago. For the most part silver no longer circulates since its bullion value now exceeds its face value. Generally speaking, the only pre-1968 coins in circulation are one-cent and five-cent pieces, and these seldom pre-date 1953. Older coins must now be purchased through dealers.

BUYING AND SELLING PRICES

Buying prices are what dealers pay for coins. Selling prices are what dealers charge for coins. Generally, dealers will pay 40% to 60% of their selling price. It should be remembered, all dealers will pay according to their needs. They will pay well for what they need immediately, but for those coins for which there is no demand, even if they have a high retail value, they will offer substantially less.

The prices shown in this book represent averages or estimates of buying prices, and should serve as a guide in negotiating fair prices when buying or selling. Also a clearer idea of what coins are in demand by collectors and dealers can be developed by studying the guide.

Coins should not be mailed for appraisal unless a written response to an inquiry is received from the dealer. If coins are mailed, then they should be sent by registered mail, insured, accompanied by a list of the coins sent, and with a complete return address and return postage.

HANDLING AND CLEANING COINS

Coins should be handled by the edges only. Avoid touching the surfaces. Many collectors have found too late that fingerprints cannot be removed from coins or other metal valuables. Proof and Specimen quality coins must be handled with extra care since their high lustre is very fragile.

Inevitably, the question of whether to clean coins or not will arise. Probably the best course to follow is, when in doubt - don't, until you have contacted an experienced collector or dealer.

The tarnish on silver coins can be removed, but it will not necessarily raise the value. If the tarnish is very thick, then its removal could leave the coin looking much worse.

Nickel coins seldom require cleaning, and only soap and water are safe since nickel is a fairly active metal. Copper and bronze should not be cleaned by anyone who is not knowledgeable in the chemical properties of these metals and their alloys.

Whatever the metal, abrasives must never be used. There are many polishes on the market which are designed for silverware, copper and brass. These must not be used with coins. The results are disastrous

HANDLING AND CLEANING PAPER MONEY

Inexperienced collectors should always use great care when handling notes. Notes should be handled as little as possible, since oil and perspiration from one's skin can damage and devalue a note. Care should be taken to ensure that unfolded or uncreased notes remain so, and that even marginals tears or abrasions are avoided. Under no circumstances should one ever wash or otherwise try to clean a note since it is likely that the note's value will be considerably reduced. The same is true for ironing or pressing. It should be avoided.

MINT MARKS

A mint mark is a letter stamped on a coin to designate the mint that produced the coins. Canadian decimal coinage issued prior to 1908 was struck at either the Tower Mint, London, in which case it had no mint mark, or at the Heaton Mint in Birmingham. The Birmingham coins had a small "H" as a mint mark. Since 1908 all Canadian coins have been struck at the Ottawa or Winnipeg Mints, with no mint marks, except the Canadian sovereigns which were identified by a small "C" above the date.

Newfoundland's coinage was struck at either London, Birmingham, or Ottawa. The Tower Mint coins had no marks, the Birmingham coins had an "H", and the Ottawa coins had a "C", except for the 1940 and 1942 cent pieces.

New Brunswick's and Nova Scotia's coinage had no mint marks because it was struck at the Tower Mint.

Prince Edward Island's coinage was struck at Birmingham but no mint mark was used because the dies were supplied by the Tower Mint.

NOVA SCOTIA

VICTORIA 1861 - 1864

Date and Denomination	Buying Price
1861 half cent	1.75
1864 half cent	1.75
1861 one cent	.50
1862 one cent	10.00
1864 one cent	.50

PRINCE EDWARD ISLAND

VICTORIA 1871

Date and Denomination	Buying Price
1871 one cent	.50

NEW BRUNSWICK

VICTORIA 1861 - 1864

Date and Denomination	Buying Price
1861 half cent	25.00
1861 one cent	.50
1864 one cent	.50
1862 five cents	15.00
1864 five cents	15.00
1862 ten cents	12.50
1864 ten cents	12.50
1862 twenty cents	7.00
1864 twenty cents	7.00

IMPORTANT
Buying prices are listed for coins graded VG or better. Bent, damaged or badly worn coins are not collectable and bring no premium value.

IMPORTANT
Do not clean your coins. Coins should be handled carefully. Only experts should consider cleaning. If you are not an expert the results can be disastrous.

NEWFOUNDLAND

LARGE CENTS

Wide O   Narrow O

GEORGE V 1913 - 1936

Date and Mint Mark	Description	Buying Price
1913		.15
1917C		.15
1919C		.15
1920C		.15
1929		.15
1936		.15

VICTORIA 1865 - 1896

Date and Mint Mark	Description	Buying Price
1865		.50
1872H		.50
1873		.50
1876H		.50
1880	Wide O	.50
1880	Narrow O	30.00
1885		5.00
1888		5.00
1890		.50
1894		.50
1896		.50

SMALL CENTS

GEORGE VI 1938 - 1948

Date and Mint Mark	Description	Buying Price
1938		.10
1940		.10
1941C		.10
1942		.10
1943C		.10
1944C		.10
1947C		.10

FIVE CENTS

EDWARD VII 1904 - 1909

Date and Mint Mark	Description	Buying Price
1904H		2.00
1907		.40
1909		.40

VICTORIA 1865 - 1896

Date and Mint Mark	Description	Buying Price
1865		9.00
1870		12.00
1872H		9.00
1873		12.00

Date and Mint Mark	Description	Buying Price
1873H		400.00
1876H		30.00
1880		7.00
1881		5.00
1882H		4.00
1885		35.00
1888		8.00
1890		2.00
1894		2.00
1896		1.00

EDWARD VII 1903 - 1908

Date and Mint Mark	Description	Buying Price
1903		1.00
1904H		1.00
1908		1.00

GEORGE V 1912 - 1929

Date and Mint Mark	Description	Buying Price
1912		.50
1917C		.50
1919C		.50
1929		.50

GEORGE VI 1938 - 1947

Date and Mint Mark	Description	Buying Price
1938		.25
1940C		.25
1941C		.25
1942C		.25
1943C		.25
1944C		.25
1945C		.25
1946C		75.00
1947C		.25

TEN CENTS

VICTORIA 1865 - 1896

Date and Mint Mark	Description	Buying Price
1865		4.00
1870		50.00
1872H		4.00
1873		5.00
1876H		8.00
1880		8.00
1882H		5.00
1885		20.00
1888		4.00
1890		1.50
1894		1.50
1896		1.25

EDWARD VII 1903 - 1904

Date and Mint Mark	Description	Buying Price
1903		.50
1904H		.50

GEORGE V 1912 -1919

Date and Mint Mark	Description	Buying Price
1912		.20
1917C		.20
1919C		.20

IMPORTANT

Buying prices are listed for coins graded VG or better. Bent, damaged or badly worn coins are not collectable and bring no premium value.

GEORGE VI 1938 - 1947

Date and Mint Mark	Description	Buying Price
1938		.20
1940		.20
1941C		.20
1942C		.20
1943C		.20
1944C		.20
1945C		.20
1946C		.20
1947C		.20

TWENTY CENTS

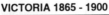

VICTORIA 1865 - 1900

Date and Mint Mark	Description	Buying Price
1865		4.00
1870		5.00
1872H		2.00
1873		3.00
1876H		4.00
1880		5.00
1881		1.50
1882H		1.00
1885		2.00
1888		1.00
1890		1.00
1894		1.00
1896		.50
1899		.50
1900		.50

IMPORTANT

Mint marks are a letter stamped on a coin to designate the mint that produced the coin. The Canadian Mint used the letter "C", while the Heaton Mint in England used the letter "H".

EDWARD VII 1904

Date and Mint Mark	Description	Buying Price
1904H		.50

GEORGE V 1912

Date and Mint Mark	Description	Buying Price
1912		.40

TWENTY-FIVE CENTS

GEORGE V 1917 - 1919

Date and Mint Mark	Description	Buying Price
1917C		.50
1919C		.50

IMPORTANT

Buying prices are listed for coins graded VG or better. Bent, damaged or badly worn coins are not collectable and bring no premium.

FIFTY CENTS

VICTORIA 1870 - 1900

Date and Mint Mark	Description	Buying Price
1870		4.00
1872H		4.00
1873		7.50
1874		4.00
1876H		6.00
1880		6.00
1881		4.00
1882H		4.00
1885		4.00
1888		5.00
1894		1.00
1896		1.00
1898		1.00
1899		1.00
1900		1.00

GEORGE V 1911 - 1919

Date and Mint Mark	Description	Buying Price
1911		.90
1917C		.90
1918C		.90
1919C		.90

TWO DOLLARS GOLD

VICTORIA 1865 - 1868

Date and Mint Mark	Description	Buying Price
1865		100.00
1870		125.00
1872		150.00
1880		500.00
1881		100.00
1882H		100.00
1885		100.00
1888		100.00

EDWARD VII 1904 - 1909

Date and Mint Mark	Description	Buying Price
1904H		.90
1907		.90
1908		.90
1909		.90

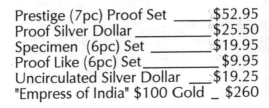

PROVINCE OF CANADA

LARGE CENTS

VICTORIA 1858 - 1859

Date and Mint Mark	Description	Buying Price
1858		15.00
1859		.50
1859	W/9 over 8	10.00

FIVE CENTS

Large Date	Small Date

VICTORIA 1858

Date and Mint Mark	Description	Buying Price
1858	Small Date	3.00
1858	Large Date	40.00

IMPORTANT

Mint marks are a letter stamped on a coin to designate the mint that produced the coin. The Canadian Mint used the letter "C", while the Heaton Mint in England used the letter "H".

TEN CENTS

VICTORIA 1858

Date and Mint Mark	Description	Buying Price
1858		4.00

TWENTY CENTS

VICTORIA 1858

Date and Mint Mark	Description	Buying Price
1858		25.00

IMPORTANT

The buying prices for silver coins are based on their intrinsic value. All issues from 1902 to 1968 are priced at the market value for $5.50 (Can. Funds) silver. Conditions play an important part in the buying price for coins between 1902 and 1936. Higher or lower silver prices will change the listed values.

IMPORTANT

Buying prices are listed for coins graded VG or better. Bent, damaged or badly worn coins are not collectable and bring no premium value.

DOMINION OF CANADA

LARGE CENTS

Large Date, Large Leaves

Small Date, Small Leaves

EDWARD VII 1902 - 1910

Date and Mint Mark	Description	Buying Price
1902		.30
1903		.30
1904		.30
1905		.30
1906		.30
1907		.30
1907H		2.00
1908		.30
1909		.30
1910		.30

VICTORIA 1876 - 1901

Date and Mint Mark	Description	Buying Price
1876H		.50
1881H		.50
1882H		.50
1884		.50
1886		.50
1887		.50
1888		.50
1890H		.50
1891	Large Leaves, Large Date	1.25
1891	Large Leaves, Small Date	20.00
1891	Small Leaves, Small Date	12.50
1892		.50
1893		.50
1894		.50
1895		.50
1896		.50
1897		.50
1898H		.50
1899		.50
1900		.50
1900H		.50
1901		.50

Large Cents were not issued for the years omitted in this listing.

GEORGE V 1911 - 1902

Date and Mint Mark	Description	Buying Price
1911		.15
1912		.15
1913		.15
1914		.15
1915		.15
1916		.15
1917		.15
1918		.15
1919		.15
1920		.15

IMPORTANT

Buying prices are listed for coins graded VG or better. Bent, damaged or badly worn coins are not collectable and bring no premium value.

SMALL CENTS

GEORGE V 1920 - 1936

Date and Mint Mark	Description	Buying Price
1920		.03
1921		.03
1922		2.50
1923		6.50
1924		1.00
1925		3.50
1926		.50
1927		.15
1928		.03
1929		.03
1930		.30
1931		.10
1932 to 1936		.03

No Shoulder Fold   Shoulder Fold

ELIZABETH II 1953 To date

Date and Mint Mark	Description	Buying Price
1953	NSF	.01
1953	SF	.05
1954 to 1964		.01

1937 Obverse   1937 Reverse

1947 Maple Leaf

GEORGE VI 1937 - 1952

Date and Mint Mark	Description	Buying Price
1937 to 1947		.01
1947	Maple Leaf	.01

In 1948 "ET IND:IMP." ceased to appear on the coinage.

Date and Mint Mark	Description	Buying Price
1948 to 1952		.01

Date and Mint Mark	Description	Buying Price
1965		.01
1966		.01
1967	Centennial	.01
1968 to 1981		.01

Date and Mint Mark	Description	Buying Price
1982 to 1989		.01

16

Date and Mint Mark	Description	Buying Price
1990 to 1992		.01

FIVE CENTS SILVER

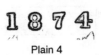
1900 Small Date

1900 Large Date

Plain 4

Crosslet 4

VICTORIA 1870 - 1901

Date and Mint Mark	Description	Buying Price
1870		2.50
1871		2.50
1872H		2.00
1874H	Plain 4	5.00
1874H	Crosslet 4	3.00
1875H	Large Date	35.00
1875H	Small Date	30.00
1880H		1.00
1881h		1.00
1882H		1.00
1883H		4.00
1884		30.00
1885		2.00
1886		1.00
1887		4.00
1888		1.00
1889		6.00
1890H		1.00
1891		1.00
1892		1.00
1893		1.00
1894		4.00
1896		1.00
1897		1.00

Date and Mint Mark	Description	Buying Price
1898		2.50
1899		1.00
1900	Large Date	4.00
1900	Small Date	.75
1901		.75

Small H   Large H

EDWARD VII 1902 - 1910

Date and Mint Mark	Description	Buying Price
1902	Plain	.40
1902	Large H	.50
1902	Small H	3.00
1903		1.00
1903H		.40
1904		.40
1905		.40
1906		.40
1907		.40
1908		1.00
1909		.40
1910		.40

GEORGE V 1911 - 1921

Date and Mint Mark	Description	Buying Price
1911		.25
1912		.25
1913		.25
1914		.30
1915		2.00
1916		.50
1917		.25
1918		.25
1919		.25
1920		.25
1921		600.00

FIVE CENTS NICKEL

Near 6   Far 6

GEORGE V 1922 - 1936

Date and Mint Mark	Description	Buying Price
1922 to 1924		.06
1925		10.00
1926	Near 6	.25
1926	Far 6	30.00
1927 to 1936		.06

Tombac Beaver

Tombac "V"   1947 Maple Leaf

GEORGE VI 1937 - 1952

Date and Mint Mark	Description	Buying Price
1937	Dot	.05
1938 to 1941		.05
1942	Nickel	.05
1942	Tombac Beaver	.07
1943	Tombac V	.07
1944 to 1945	Steel V	.05
1946 to 1947		.05
1947	Maple Leaf	.05

In 1948 "ET IND:IMP." ceased to appear on the coinage.

Date and Mint Mark	Description	Buying Price
1948 to 1950		.05

1951 Beaver   1951 Commemorative

Date and Mint Mark	Description	Buying Price
1951	Commemorative	.05
1951	Beaver	.05
1952		.05

ELIZABETH II 1953 to date

Date and Mint Mark	Description	Buying Price
1953 to 1966		.05
1967	Centennial	.05
1968 to 1989		.05

Date and Mint Mark	Description	Buying Price
1990 to 1992		.05

TEN CENTS

Flat Top 3   Round Top 3

VICTORIA 1970 - 1901

Date and Mint Mark	Description	Buying Price
1870		3.00
1871		4.00
1871H		5.00
1872H		20.00
1874H		2.00
1875H		60.00
1880H		2.00
1881H		2.50
1882H		2.00
1883H		5.00
1884		45.00
1885		4.00
1886		4.00
1887		5.00
1888		2.00
1889		125.00
1890H		3.00
1891		3.00
1892		2.50
1893	Flat Top 3	4.00
1893	Round Top 3	150.00
1894		2.50
1896		2.00
1898		2.00
1899		2.00
1900		1.00
1901		1.00

EDWARD VII 1902 - 1910

Date and Mint Mark	Description	Buying Price
1902		.50
1902H		.50
1903		.50
1903H		.50
1904		.50
1905		.50
1906		.50
1907		.50
1908		.50
1909		.50
1910		.50

Small Leaves   Broad Leaves

GEORGE V 1911 - 1936

Date and Mint Mark	Description	Buying Price
1911		2.00
1912		.17
1913	Broad Leaves	35.00
1913	Small Leaves	.17
1914 to 1936		.17

GEORGE VI 1937 - 1952

Date and Mint Mark	Description	Buying Price
1937 to 1947		.17
1947	Maple Leaf	.17

In 1948 "ET IND:IMP." ceased to appear on coinage.

Date and Mint Mark	Description	Buying Price
1948		.75
1949 to 1952		.17

1969 Small Date   1969 Large Date

ELIZABETH II 1952 to date

Date and Mint Mark	Description	Buying Price
1953 to 1966		.17
1967	Centennial	.14
1968	.500 Fine	.12
1968	Nickel	.10
1969	Large Date	3,000.00
1969	Small Date	.10
1970 to 1989		.10

Date and Mint Mark	Description	Buying Price
1990 to 1992		.10

TWENTY-FIVE CENTS

Narrow O   Wide O

VICTORIA 1870 - 1901

Date and Mint Mark	Description	Buying Price
1870		3.00
1871		4.00
1871H		5.00
1872H		2.00
1874H		2.00
1875H		100.00
1880H	Narrow O	11.00
1880H	Wide O	30.00
1881H		3.00
1882H		4.00
1883H		3.00
1885		25.00
1886		3.00
1887		25.00
1888		4.00
1889		30.00
1890H		5.00
1891		15.00
1892		3.00
1893		22.00
1894		4.00
1899		2.00
1900		1.00
1901		2.00

EDWARD VII 1902 - 1910

Date and Mint Mark	Description	Buying Price
1902		.75
1902H		.75
1903		.75
1904		4.00
1905		.75
1906		.75
1907		.75
1908		.75
1909		.75
1910		.75

In 1948 "ET IND"IMP." ceased to appear on the coinage.

Date and Mint Mark	Description	Buying Price
1948 to 1952		.45

Obverse 1953-64	Obverse 1965-1989

GEORGE V 1911- 1936

Date and Mint Mark	Description	Buying Price
1911		3.00
1912 to 1914		.45
1915		5.00
1916 to 1920		.45
1921		3.00
1927		9.00
1928 to 1936		.45
1936	Dot	25.00

Reverse 1953-89	Reverse 1967

ELIZABETH II 1953 to date

Date and Mint Mark	Description	Buying Price
1953	Large Date	.45
1953	Small Date	.45
1954 to 1966		.45
1967	Centennial	.35
1968	.500 Fine	.30
1968	Nickel	.25

IMPORTANT

Do not clean your coins. Coins should be handled carefully. Only experts should consider cleaning. If you are not an expert the results can be disastrous.

GEORGE VI 1937 - 1952

Date and Mint Mark	Description	Buying Price
1937 to 1947		.45
1947	Maple Leaf	.45

Large Bust
132 Obverse Beads

Small Bust
120 Obverse Beads

FIFTY CENTS

L.C.W.   No L.C.W.

Date and Mint Mark	Description	Buying Price
1973	Small Bust	.25
1973	Large Bust	20.00
1974 to 1989		.25

VICTORIA 1870 - 1901

Date and Mint Mark	Description	Buying Price
1870	Without L.C.W.	250.00
1870	With L.C.W.	12.00
1871		16.00
1871H		25.00
1872H		12.00
1881H		12.00
1888		35.00
1890H		350.00
1892		16.00
1894		75.00
1898		14.00
1899		22.00
1900		9.00
1901		10.00

Date and Mint Mark	Description	Buying Price
1990 to 1992		.25

IMPORTANT

Buying prices are listed for coins graded VG or better. Bent, damaged or badly worn coins are not collectable and bring no premium value.

EDWARD VII 1902 - 1910

Date and Mint Mark	Description	Buying Price
1902		5.00
1903H		6.00
1904		30.00
1905		40.00

Date and Mint Mark	Description	Buying Price
1906		5.00
1907		4.00
1908		.90
1909		.90
1910		.90

Maple Leaf   No Maple Leaf
1947 Straight "7"

Maple Leaf   No Maple Leaf
1947 Curved "7"

GEORGE V 1911 - 1936

Date and Mint Mark	Description	Buying Price
1911 to 1920		.90
1921*		4,000.00
1929		.90
1931		.90
1932		15.00
1934		5.00
1936		4.00

*Majority were melted down, approximately 75 are known. Beware of altered date.

Date and Mint Mark	Description	Buying Price
1947	Straight "7"	.90
1947	Curved "7"	.90
1947	M.L., Straight "7"	6.00
1947	M.L., Curved "7"	600.00

In 1948 "ET IND:IMP." ceased to appear on the coinage

Date and Mint Mark	Description	Buying Price
1948		15.00
1949 to 1952		.90

GEORGE VI 1937 - 1952

Date and Mint Mark	Description	Buying Price
1937 to 1946		.90

IMPORTANT

Do not clean your coins. Coins should be handled carefully. Only experts should consider cleaning. If you are not an expert the results can be disastrous.

No Shoulder Fold   Shoulder Fold

Date and Mint Mark	Description	Buying Price
1968 to 1989		.50

Small Date   Large Date

ELIZABETH II 1953 to date

Date and Mint Mark	Description	Buying Price
1953	SD, NSF	.90
1953	LD, NSF	2.00
1953	LD, SF	.90
1954 to 1964		.90

Date and Mint Mark	Description	Buying Price
1990 to 1992		.50

Date and Mint Mark	Description	Buying Price
1965 to 1966		.90
1967	Centennial	.90

SILVER DOLLARS

1935 Obverse

1936 Obverse

1937 to 1947 Obverse

1935 Reverse

1939 Parliament

1949 Newfoundland

1947   **1947**

1947 Blunt 7   1947 Pointed 7

1952 Waterlines

1952 No Waterlines

1947.

1947 Maple Leaf

GEORGE V 1935 - 1936

Date and Mint Mark	Description	Buying Price
1935	Silver Jubilee	30.00
1936	Voyageur	10.00

GEORGE VI 1937 - 1952

Date and Mint Mark	Description	Buying Price
1937	Voyageur	10.00
1938	Voyageur	25.00
1939	Royal Visit	10.00
1945	Voyageur	50.00
1946	Voyageur	12.00
1947	Blunt 7	30.00

Date and Mint Mark	Description	Buying Price
1947	Pointed 7	60.00
1947	Maple Leaf	75.00
1948	Dei Gratia	400.00
1949	Newfoundland	10.00
1950	Voyageur	5.00
1950	Arnprior	5.00
1951	Voyageur	5.00
1951	Arnprior	20.00
1952	Waterlines	4.00
1952	No Waterlines	4.00

Arnprior dollars are known to exist in the years 1950, 1951 and 1955. Other years may contain Arnpriors but are not known to exist.

| Obverse | 1953 | Reverse | 1964 Charlottetown |

| 1958 British Columbia | 1965 Obverse | 1967 Centennial |

| 1955 No Water Lines | 1955 1 1/2 Waterlines |

ELIZABETH II 1953 to date

Date and Mint Mark	Description	Buying Price	Date and Mint Mark	Description	Buying Price
1953	Voyageur	2.50	1960	Voyageur	2.50
1954	Voyageur	2.50	1961	Voyageur	2.50
1955	Voyageur	2.50	1962	Voyageur	2.50
1955	Arnprior	40.00	1963	Voyageur	2.50
1956	Voyageur	2.50	1964	Charlottetown	2.50
1957	Voyageur	2.50	1965	Voyageur	2.50
1957	One Waterline	2.50	1966	Voyageur	2.50
1958	British Columbia	2.50	1967	Centennial	2.50
1959	Voyageur	2.50			

IMPORTANT

Do not clean your coins. Coins should be handled carefully. Only experts should consider cleaning. If you are not an expert the results can be disastrous.

IMPORTANT

The Silver Dollar buying prices are for problem free coins in very fine condition. Damaged coins will bring lower prices

NICKEL DOLLARS

1968 to 1987 Obverse   Reverse

Manitoba   British Columbia   Prince Edward Island

Winnipeg   Constitution   Jacques Cartier

Date and Mint Mark	Description	Buying Price	Date and Mint Mark	Description	Buying Price
1968	Voyageur	1.00	1975 to 1981	Voyageur	1.00
1969	Voyageur	1.00	1982	Constitution	1.00
1970	Manitoba	1.00	1983	Voyageur	1.00
1971	British Columbia	1.00	1984	Jacques Cartier	1.00
1972	Voyageur	1.00	1985	Voyageur	1.00
1973	P.E.I.	1.00	1986	Voyageur	1.00
1974	Winnipeg	1.00	1987	Voyageur	1.00

	Loon			Loon	
Obverse		Reverse	Obverse		Reverse

Date and Mint Mark	Description	Buying Price	Date and Mint Mark	Description	Buying Price
1987 to 1989	Loon	1.00	1990 to 1992	Loon	1.00

GOLD COINS

SOVEREIGNS

EDWARD VII 1908 - 1910

Date and Mint Mark	Description	Buying Price
1908C		900.00
1909C		140.00
1910C		140.00

GEORGE V 1911 - 1919

Date and Mint Mark	Description	Buying Price
1911C		90.00
1913C		200.00
1914C		150.00
1916C		5,000.00
1917C		90.00
1918C		90.00
1919C		90.00

FIVE DOLLARS

GEORGE V 1912 - 1914

Date and Mint Mark	Description	Buying Price
1912		125.00
1913		125.00
1914		250.00

TEN DOLLARS

GEORGE V 1912 - 1914

Date and Mint Mark	Description	Buying Price
1912		250.00
1913		250.00
1914		300.00

TWENTY DOLLARS

ELIZABETH II 1953 to date

Date and Mint Mark	Description	Buying Price
1967	Centennial	190.00
1967	Complete Set	200.00

IMPORTANT

Do not clean your coins, Coins should be handled carefully. Only experts should consider cleaning. If you are not an expert the results can be disastrous

ONE HUNDRED DOLLARS

Canada issued the first one hundred dollar gold coin in 1976 to commemorate the Montreal Olympic Games. In that year two qualities and fineness were released, uncirculated - .585 fine (14 karat) and proof - .900 fine. From 1976 to 1986 only proof quality coins with a fineness of .925 were issued. In 1987 the quality remained the same (proof) but the fineness of the coin was altered to .585 fine or 14 karat, again.

IMPORTANT

Proof coins must be in mint state condition. Mishandled, mounted or damaged coins are discounted from the prices listed. The buying price for gold coins is tied to the market price of gold. Any movement on the gold price will result in a corresponding price movement in these coins.

1976 - 14 kt   1976 - 22 kt

1977   1978   1979   1980

1981   1982   1983   1984

Date	Description	Fineness	Buying Price	Date	Description	Fineness	Buying Price
1976	14 kt Olympic	.585	100.00	1980	Arctic Territories	.925	180.00
1976	22 kt Olympic	.900	180.00	1981	"O" Canada	.925	180.00
1977	Jubilee	.925	180.00	1982	Constitution	.925	180.00
1978	Unity	.925	180.00	1983	Gilbert's Landing	.925	185.00
1979	Year of the Child	.925	180.00	1984	Voyage of Discovery	.925	195.00

ONE HUNDRED DOLLARS

1985	1986	1987 - 14 kt	1988 - 14 kt

1989 - 14 kt	1990 - 14 kt	1991 - 14 kt

Date	Description	Fineness	Buying Price	Date	Description	Fineness	Buying Price
1985	National Parks	.925	190.00	1988	Bowhead Whale	.585	200.00
1986	Peace	.925	185.00	1989	Ste. Marie	.585	175.00
1987	Winter Olympic Games	.585	175.00	1990	Literacy Year	.585	175.00
				1991	Empress of India	.585	175.00

MAPLE LEAF BULLION COINS

The Maple Leaf gold coins were first produced in 1979, the fractional or small sizes three years later in 1982 and the half ounce size in 1986. In 1988 platinum and silver coins were issued to complete the precious metal bullion series.

The Maple Leaf bullion coins are purchased based on the spot market on the day of purchase times their gold content less a small handling charge.

$50	$20	$10	$5

PLATINUM AND GOLD CONTENTS

1/10 Maple Leaf	$5 - 0.10 Troy ounce	1/2 Maple Leaf	$20 - 0.50 Troy ounce
1/4 Maple Leaf	$10 - 0.25 Troy ounce	Maple Leaf	$50 - 1.00 Troy ounce

SILVER CONTENT
Maple Leaf $5 - 1.00 Troy Ounce

COLLECTORS ISSUES

The Numismatic department of the Royal Canadian Mint issued specially struck and packaged coins starting in 1954. The coins were issued for collectors and as a result are of high quality. The dealer buying prices listed below are for single coins and sets in their original packaging and condition. Coins or sets which have been mishandled or damaged are discounted from the prices listed. Beginning in 1961 the Numismatic Department of the Royal Canadian Mint issued silver dollars for collectors in two conditions, proof and uncirculated. Proof condition dollars were issued in black leatherette boxes and uncirculated dollars were issued in a clear plastic container.

SILVER PROOF-LIKE DOLLARS

Date	Description	Buying Price	Date	Description	Buying Price
1954	Voyageur	175.00	1959	Voyageur	10.00
1955	Voyageur	120.00	1960	Voyageur	6.00
1955	Arnprior	175.00	1961	Voyageur	3.00
1956	Voyageur	75.00	1962	Voyageur	2.50
1957	Voyageur	30.00	1963	Voyageur	2.50
1958	British Columbia	20.00	1964	Charlottetown	2.50

CASED NICKEL DOLLARS

Manitoba

British Columbia

Prince Edward Island

Winnipeg

Constitution

Jaques Cartier

Date	Description	Buying Price	Date	Description	Buying Price
1970	Manitoba	1.00	1975	Voyageur	1.00
1971	British Columbia	1.00	1976	Voyageur	1.00
1972	Voyageur	1.00	1982	Constitution	3.00
1973	Prince Edward Island	1.00	1984	Jacques Cartier	3.00
1974	Winnipeg	1.00	1987	Loon	10.00

CASED SILVER DOLLARS

1971 British Columbia

1973 R.C.M.P.   1974 Winnpeg   1975 Calgary

1976 Parliament   1977 Jubilee

Date	Description	Buying Price	Date	Description	Buying Price
1971	British Columbia	6.00	1975	Calgary Stampede	4.50
1972	Voyageur	4.00	1976	Library of Parliament	8.00
1973	R.C.M.P.	6.00	1977	Jubilee	6.00
1974	Winnipeg	6.00			

1978 Commonwealth Games

1979 Griffon

Arctic Territories

1981 Trans Canada

1982 Regina

1983 University Games

Date	Description	Buying Price	Date	Description	Buying Price
1978	Commonwealth Games	4.00	1982	Regina (PF)	4.00
1979	Griffon	13.00	1982	Regina (UNC)	20.00
1980	Arctic Territories	30.00	1983	University Games (PF)	7.00
1981	Trans Canada (PF)	14.00	1983	University Games (UNC)	20.00
1981	Trans Canada (UNC)	25.00			

1984 Toronto

1985 National Parks

1986 Vancouver   1987 Davis Strait

Date	Description	Buying Price	Date	Description	Buying Price
1984	Toronto (PF)	5.00	1986	Vancouver (PF)	7.00
1984	Toronto (UNC)	20.00	1986	Vancouver (UNC)	20.00
1985	National Parks (PF)	5.00	1987	Davis Strait (PF)	11.00
1985	National Parks (UNC)	20.00	1987	Davis Strait (UNC)	20.00

1988 Ironworks   1989 MacKenzie River

1990 Henry Kelsey

1991 Frontenac

Date	Description	Buying Price	Date	Description	Buying Price
1988	Ironworks (PF)	12.00	1991	Frontenac (PF)	12.00
1988	Ironworks (UNC)	15.00	1991	Frontenac (UNC)	10.00
1989	MacKenzie River (PF)	12.00	1992	(PF)	12.00
1989	MacKenzie River (UNC)	15.00	1992	(UNC)	10.00
1990	Henry Kelsey (PF)	12.00			
1990	Henry Kelsey (UNC)	10.00			

SILVER PROOF-LIKE SETS

Date	Description	Buying Price
1954	Voyageur	200.00
1955	Voyageur	150.00
1955	Arnprior	200.00
1956	Voyageur	85.00
1957	Voyageur	45.00
1958	British Columbia	35.00
1959	Voyageur	20.00
1960	Voyageur	10.00
1961	Voyageur	5.00
1962	Voyageur	5.00
1963	Voyageur	5.00
1964	Charlottetown	5.00
1965	Voyageur	5.00
1966	Voyageur	5.00
1967	Centennial	5.00

NICKEL PROOF-LIKE SETS

Date	Description	Buying Price
1968	Voyageur	2.00
1969	Voyageur	2.00
1970	Manitoba	2.00
1971	British Columbia	2.00
1972	Voyageur	2.00
1973	R.C.M.P., Small Bust	2.00
1973	R.C.M.P., Large Bust	75.00
1974	Winnipeg	2.00
1975	Voyageur	2.00
1976	Voyageur	2.00
1977	Voyageur	2.00
1978	Voyageur	2.00
1979	Voyageur	2.00
1980	Voyageur	3.00
1981	Voyageur	2.50
1982	Voyageur	2.00
1983	Voyageur	5.00
1984	Voyageur	3.00
1985	Voyageur	5.00
1986	Voyageur	10.00
1987	Voyageur	4.00
1988	Loon	4.00
1989	Loon	4.00
1990	Loon	4.00
1991	Loon	4.00
1992	Loon	4.00

CUSTOM SETS

Issued by the Royal Canadian Mint between 1971 and 1980, contains 1-cent to the nickel dollar plus an extra cent (7 coins).

Date	Description	Buying Price
1971 to 1980		2.00

SPECIMEN SETS

Issued by the Royal Canadian Mint starting in 1981 and continuing to date, contains 1-cent to the nickel dollar (6 coins).

Date	Description	Buying Price
1981	Voyageur	5.00
1982	Voyageur	5.00
1983	Voyageur	5.00
1984	Voyageur	5.00
1985	Voyageur	5.00
1986	Voyageur	5.00
1987	Voyageur	5.00
1988	Loon	5.00
1989	Loon	5.00
1990	Loon	5.00
1991	Loon	5.00
1992	Loon	5.00

PRESTIGE PROOF SETS

Issued by the Royal Canadian Mint in 1971 and continuing to date, contains 1-cent to the nickel dollar plus the silver dollar of that year (7 coins).

Date	Description	Buying Price
1971		7.00
1972		10.00
1973	Small Bust	7.00
1973	Large Bust	100.00
1974		6.00
1975		6.00
1976		7.00
1977		7.00
1978		7.00
1979		8.00
1980		35.00
1981		25.00
1982		7.00
1983		7.00
1984		10.00
1985		10.00
1986		12.00
1987		15.00
1988		15.00
1989		25.00
1990		25.00
1991		25.00
1992		25.00

SPECIMEN SETS

Sets of Specimen coins have been issued in Canada at various times since 1858, often in official cases. A representative selection follows. Sets from 1908 are in leather or leatherette covered presentation cases.

Date	Description	Buying Price
1858	Victoria:	
	1, 5, 10, 20 cents	1,500.00
1870	Victoria:	
	5, 10, 25, 50 cents	3,000.00
1908	Edward VII:	
	1, 5, 10, 25, 50 cents	500.00

Date	Description	Buying Price
1911	George V:	
	1, 5, 10, 25, 50 cents	2,000.00
1937	George VI:	
	1, 5, 10, 25, 50 cents $1	400.00
1937	George VI:	
	as above, but in card case	300.00
1967	Elizabeth II: Centennial,	
	1, 5, 10, 25, 50 cents	
	$1.00, $20.00 gold	232.00
1967	Elizabeth: Centennial,	
	as above, but with medal	
	instead of $20.00 gold	10.00

1976 MONTREAL OLYPMIC COINS

For the Summer Olympic Games of 1976, held in Montreal, seven series of silver coins were minted. There were four different coins in each series. Two $5 and two $10 coins, struck in sterling silver. The $5 coins weigh 24.3 grams and the $10 coins weigh 48.6 grams. The coins were available, encapsulated in plastic, as single coins, and in Custom, Prestige and Proof four coin sets. Each set of four coins, $30.00, contains 4.28 oz. of fine silver. The purchase price of these sets is linked to the market price of silver, even if the intrinsic value falls below the face value. Large quantities of these coins were issued and they are not redeemable by the government or the banks.

SERIES I

$5 Map of North America

$5 Kingston

$10 World Map

$10 Montreal

SERIES II

$5 Athlete with Torch

$5 Olive Wreath

$10 Head of Zeus

$10 Temple of Zeus

SERIES III

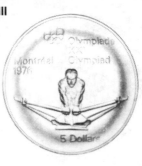

$5 Canoeing

$ 5 Rowing

$10 Lacrosse

$10 Bicycling

SERIES IV

$5 The Marathon

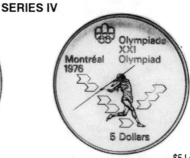

$5 Ladies' Javelin

$10 Men's Hurdles

$10 Ladies' Shot Put

SERIES V

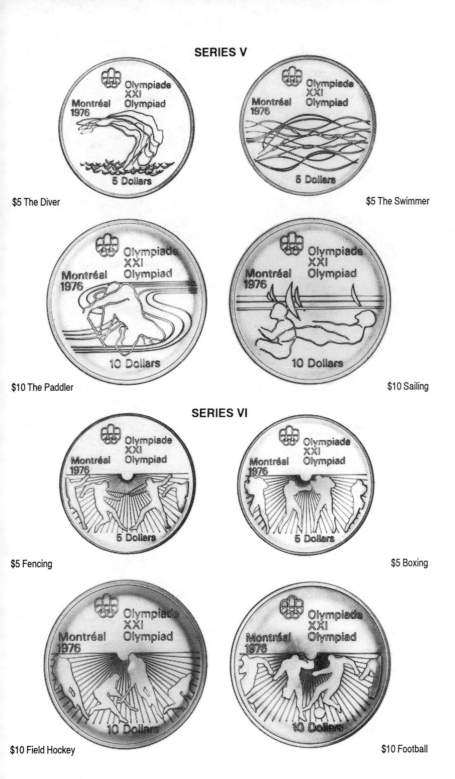

$5 The Diver

$5 The Swimmer

$10 The Paddler

$10 Sailing

SERIES VI

$5 Fencing

$5 Boxing

$10 Field Hockey

$10 Football

SERIES VII

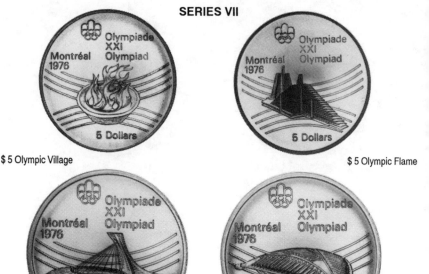

$ 5 Olympic Village

$ 5 Olympic Flame

$10 Olympic Stadium

$10 Olympic Velodrome

Date	Series	$5 Coin	$10 Coin	Custom Set	Prestige Set	Proof Set
1973	1	3.50	7.00	21.00	21.00	32.50
1974 Mule		-	100.00	-	-	-
1974	2	3.50	7.00	21.00	21.00	32.50
1974	3	3.50	7.00	21.00	21.00	32.50
1975	4	3.50	7.00	21.00	21.00	32.50
1975	5	3.50	7.00	21.00	21.00	32.50
1976	6	3.50	7.00	21.00	21.00	32.50
1976	7	3.50	7.00	21.00	21.00	32.50

1988 CALGARY OLYMPIC GAMES

The XV Winter Olympic Games were held in Calgary, February 13th to 29th, 1988. Ten different $20 silver coins were issued to commemorate this event. The coins weigh 34.107 grams, the composition is .925 silver and .075 copper, and the coins were issued in Proof-singles or Proof-Sets in one or two coin display cases. Incorporated into the design of these coins are the letters "XV OLYMPIC WINTER GAMES - XV es JEUX OLYMPIQUE D'HIVER" impressed into the edge. During the striking of these coins at the Royal Canadian Mint the impressed procedures were skipped on some series resulting in the edge lettering being missed on four known coins resulting in varieties.

FIRST SERIES

Downhill Skiing

Speed Skating

SECOND SERIES

Hockey

Biathalon

THIRD SERIES

Cross-Country Skiing

Free-Style Skiing

FOURTH SERIES

Figure Skating

Curling

FIFTH SERIES

Ski-Jumping

Bobsleigh

Date	Description	Proof Single	Proof Set
1985	Downhill Skiing	20.00	
1985	Speed Skating	20.00	40.00
1985	Speed Skating, no edge lettering	100.00	
1986	Hockey	20.00	
1986	Hockey, no edge lettering	100.00	
1986	Biathlon	20.00	40.00
1986	Biathlon, no edge lettering	100.00	
1986	Cross-Country Skiing	30.00	
1986	Free-Style Skiing	30.00	60.00
1986	Free-Style Skiing, no edge lettering	100.00	
1987	Figure Skating	30.00	
1987	Curling	30.00	60.00
1987	Ski-Jumping	30.00	
1987	Bobsleigh	30.00	60.00

PAPER MONEY OF CANADA

PROVINCE OF CANADA

1866 ISSUES

Denom.	Issue Date	Buying Price	Denom.	Issue Date	Buying Price
$1	1866	100.00	$10	1866	300.00
$2	1866	125.00	$20	1866	300.00
$5	1866	200.00	$50	1866	300.00

DOMINION OF CANADA

1870 ISSUES

Denom.		Issue Date	Buying Price
25-cent	Plain	1870	3.00
25-cent	Series A	1870	20.00
25-cent	Series B	1870	4.00

Plain   Series Letter "A"   Series Letter "B"

1870 ISSUES

Denom.	Issue Date	Variety/Signature	Buying Price
$1	1870	Payable at Montreal or Toronto	50.00
$1	1870	Payable at Halifax	125.00
$1	1870	Payable at St. John	150.00
$2	1870	Payable at Montreal or Toronto	175.00
$2	1870	Payable at Halifax or St. John	200.00

1878 ISSUES

Denom.	Issue Date	Variety/Signature	Buying Price
$1	1878	Scalloped Frame, Payable at Montreal or Toronto	55.00
$1	1878	Scalloped Frame, Payable at St. John or Halifax	100.00
$1	1878	Lettered Frame, Payable at Montreal or Toronto	10.00
$1	1878	Lettered Frame, Payable at St. John or Halifax	100.00
$2	1878	Payable at Montreal or Toronto	100.00
$2	1878	Payable at St. John or Halifax	175.00

1882 AND 1887 ISSUES

Denom.	Issue Date	Variety/Signature	Buying Price
$4	1882		50.00
$2	1887	Plain, Series A	40.00

1897 AND 1898 ISSUES

No "One"   Inward "One"   Outward "One"

Denom.	Issue Date	Variety/Signature	Buying Price
$1	1897	Green Face Tint	25.00
$2	1897	Red-Brown Back	30.00
$2	1897	Dark Brown Back	10.00
$1	1898	Inward "One"	10.00
$1	1898	Outward "One"	9.00

1900 AND 1902 ISSUES

"4" on Top   "Four" on Top

Denom.	Issue Date	Variety/Signature	Buying Price
25-cent	1900	Courtney	1.00
25-cent	1900	Bouville	1.00
25-cent	1900	Saunders	1.00
$4	1900		40.00
$4	1902	"4" on Top	50.00
$4	1902	"Four" on Top	35.00

1911 AND 1912 ISSUES

No Seal   Seal Over Five   Seal Only

Denom.	Issue Date	Variety/Signature	Buying Price
$1	1911	Green Line/Black Line Series	6.00
$500	1911		1,000.00
$1,000	1911		2,000.00
$5	1912	No Seal	12.00
$5	1912	Seal over Five	20.00
$5	1912	Seal Only	12.00

1914 AND 1917 ISSUES

Denom.	Issue Date	Variety/Signature	Buying Price
$2	1914	No Seal	7.00
$2	1914	Seal Over Two	22.00
$2	1914	Seal Only	13.00
$1	1917	No Seal	3.00
$1	1917	With Seal	5.00
$1	1917	Black Seal	5.00

1923 ISSUES

Denom.	Issue Date	Variety/Signature	Buying Price
25-cent	1923	Hyndman/Saunders	1.00
25-cent	1923	McCavour/Saunders	1.00
25-cent	1923	Campbell/Clark	1.00
$1	1923	Various Colour Seals	3.00
$1	1923	Purple Seal	25.00
$2	1923	Various Colour Seals	5.00
$2	1923	Green Seal	8.00
$2	1923	Bronze Seal	6.00

1924 AND 1925 ISSUES

Denom.	Issue Date	Variety/Signature	Buying Price
$5	1924	Queen Mary	75.00
$500	1925	George V	1,000.00
$1,000	1925	Queen Mary	2,000.00

BANK OF CANADA

1935 ISSUES

Denom.	Variety	Buying Price	Denom.	Variety	Buying Price
$1	English text	3.00	$20	French text	30.00
$1	French text	3.00	$25	English text	100.00
$2	English text	5.00	$25	French text	200.00
$2	French text	7.00	$50	English text	60.00
$5	English text	8.00	$50	French text	65.00
$5	French text	10.00	$100	English text	110.00
$10	English text	15.00	$100	French text	120.00
$10	French text	20.00	$500	English and French	550.00
$20	English text, small seal	30.00	$1,000	English and French	1,050.00

IMPORTANT

Bank notes with tears, missing corners, pinholes and folding creases are not considered to be very fine (VF). Notes in poor condition are not collectable.

Denom.	Very Fine Buying Price By Signature		
	Osborne	Gordon	Coyne
$1	2.50	1.25	1.25
$2	4.00	2.50	2.50
$5	20.00	5.25	5.25
$10	13.00	10.00	10.00
$20	23.00	20.00	20.00
$50	60.00	50.00	50.00
$100	105.00	100.00	100.00
$1,000	1,025.00	NI	NI

Note: NI-Not issued.

1954 ISSUES

"DEVIL'S FACE" PORTRAIT

IMPORTANT

The buying prices listed below are for notes in extremely fine condition. The notes must be clean with no tears, pinholes or noticeable folds or creases.

THE DEVIL'S FACE NOTES

On the earliest notes of the 1954 issue, highlighted areas of the Queen's hair produced the illusion of a leering demonic face behind her ear. This was not the result of an error, nor was it, as some have asserted, the prank of an IRA sympathizer at the bank note company. It was merely the faithful reproduction of the original photograph. The portrait of the Queen with the "Devil's Face" outlined in her hair generated almost instant controversy.

ASTERISK NOTES

Asterisk notes are replacement notes. The first being spoiled in printing, cutting, etc., and replaced by an asterisk note.
Asterisk Serial Number

| Denom. | Extremely Fine Buying Price By Signature | | | |
| | Coyne/Towers | | Beattie/Coyne | |
	Regular	Asterisk	Regular	Asterisk
$1	2.00	50.00	2.00	20.00
$2	3.00	40.00	3.50	25.00
$5	6.00	200.00	5.00	110.00
$10	11.00	50.00	10.00	40.00
$20	30.00	110.00	20.00	50.00
$50	50.00	NI	50.00	NI
$100	100.00	NI	100.00	NI
$1,000	1,025.00	NI	NI	NI

*NI-Not Issued

MODIFIED PORTRAIT

IMPORTANT
The buying prices listed below are for notes in uncirculated condition (new). The note must be clean, crisp, with no tears, creases, folds or marks of any kind or description.

MODIFIED PORTRAIT

The portrait was modified by darkening the highlights in the hair and thus removing the shading which had resulted in the "devil". The modification of the face plates was made for most denominations in 1956, except for the $1,000 denomination which was modified several years later.

| | Uncirculated Buying Price By Signature | | | | | | | |
| | Beattie/Coyne | | Beattie/Rasminsky | | Bouey/Rasminsky | | Lawson/Bouey | |
Denom.	Regular	Asterisk	Regular	Asterisk	Regular	Asterisk	Regular	Asterisk
$1	1.75	10.00	1.75	3.00	1.75	3.00	1.75	2.00
$2	6.00	20.00	2.50	4.00	2.50	3.00	2.50	4.00
$5	10.00	20.00	7.50	10.00	10.00	15.00	NI	NI
$10	15.00	25.00	12.50	15.00	NI	NI	NI	NI
$20	30.00	40.00	25.00	40.00	NI	NI	NI	NI
$50	60.00	NI	55.00	NI	NI	NI	100.00	NI
$100	105.00	NI	105.00	NI	NI	NI	105.00	NI
$1,000	1,000.00	NI	1,000.00	NI	1,000.00	NI	1,000.00	NI

*NI-Not Issued

$1 CENTENNIAL 1967

For the centennial of Canada's Confederation a special $1 note was issued. The note has a single design and two types of serial numbers, regular serial numbers and a special number 1867 - 1967. The special series was available from the Bank of Canada as a collector's item, but examples were soon found in circulation. In addition there was an asterisk note series for replacement notes.

Denom.	Issue Date	Variety	Uncirculated Buying Price
$1	1967	Commemorative serial number 1867-1967	1.00
$1	1967	Regular serial number	1.00
$1	1967	Asterisk serial number	1.50

1969 - 1975 ISSUE

This new series combined fine line engraving with subtle variations to make notes that are extremely difficult to counterfeit. The series features a new portrait of the Queen, and portraits of some of previous prime ministers of Canada.

IMPORTANT

The buying prices listed below are for notes in uncirculated condition (new). The note must be clean, crisp, with no tears, creases, folds or marks of any kind or description.

1969-1975 ISSUE

ASTERISK REPLACEMENT NOTES

Replacement of defective notes by asterisk notes was continued when the 1969-1975 issue was introduced. The highest denomination of the 1954 issue to be printed with asterisks was the $20; however, all denominations in the 1969-1975 issue including the $50 and $100 notes occur with asterisks in front of the two letter prefix type.

When the triple letter prefix notes were introduced in 1981, the use of asterisk notes was discontinued. For triple letter prefix notes, a replacement note is designated by the use of an "x" for the third letter.

Asterisk Notes	"X" Replacement Notes
BC-46aA	BC-46A-i

	Uncirculated Buying Price By Signature							
	Beattie/Rasminsky		Bouey/Rasminsky		Lawson\Bouey		Crow\Bouey	
Denom.	Regular	Asterisk	Regular	Asterisk	Regular	Asterisk	Regular	Asterisk
$1	NI	NI	NI	NI	1.25	1.50	1.00	1.50
$2	NI	NI	NI	NI	2.25	4.00	2.00	20.00
$5	NI	NI	7.50	10.00	7.00	8.00	NI	NI
$10	15.00	20.00	20.00	15.00	12.00	15.00	12.00	15.00
$20	22.00	25.00	NI	NI	22.00	25.00	NI	NI
$50	NI	NI	NI	NI	50.00	60.00	50.00	55.00
$100	NI	NI	NI	NI	100.00	105.00	100.00	105.00

Note: The Thiessen\Crow combination of signatures does not command a numismatic premium at this time.

Note: NI-Not Issued

1979 ISSUES

The series beginning in 1979 is a modification of the previous issue. The face designs are similar, as is the colouration. The serial numbers are moved to the back of the note at the bottom where the name of the Bank of Canada previously appeared. The black serial numbers are machine readable.

IMPORTANT
The buying prices listed below are for notes in uncirculated condition (new). The note must be clean, crisp, with no tears, creases, folds or marks of any kind or description.

REPLACEMENT NOTES

There are no asterisk notes in this issue. The replacement notes are designated by the second digit in the serial number.

The digit 1 following the first digit 3 of the $5 notes designates a replacement note. In the $20 denomination the replacement notes can be distinguished by "510" for the CBN company and "516" for the BABN company.

$5 Replacement note $20 Replacement note

| Denom. | Uncirculated Buying Price By Signature | | | | | |
| | Lawson\Bouey | | Crow\Bouey | | Thiessen\Crow | |
	Regular	Asterisk	Regular	Asterisk	Regular	Asterisk
$5	6.00	30.00	6.00	60.00	NI	NI
$20	25.00	30.00	20.00	25.00	20.00	25.00

1986 ISSUES

On March 14, 1986, the Bank of Canada introduced a new series of bank notes. The new designs were launched that year with the issue of the $2 and $5 notes. The Bank of Canada has not undertaken a redesign of the $1 note because of the Government of Canada's decision to introduce the one-dollar coin for circulation. The $1 note was phased out at the beginning of 1989.

Notes from 1986 to date do not command a numismatic premium above face value.

NEWFOUNDLAND
PUBLIC WORKS CASH NOTES

Denom.	Buying Price
40-cents	35.00
50-cents	35.00
80-cents	40.00
$1	50.00
$5	75.00

Denom.	Buying Price
25-cents	10.00
50-cents	10.00
$1	20.00
$2	50.00
$5	100.00

GOVERNMENT NOTES

Denom.	Buying Price
$1	8.00
$2	12.00

PRINCE EDWARD ISLAND

Denom.	Buying Price
1848-1870 £1	250.00
1872 $10	200.00
1872 $20	200.00

NOVA SCOTIA

Denom.	Buying Price
1848-1854 £1	75.00
1861 $5	100.00

COLONIAL COINS AND TOKENS

Canada has produced a great number of tokens of various kinds over the years. Tokens were used as a form of currency prior to the institution of the decimal currency system in 1858 (Colonial issues are not all tokens, some being regal coins). After Confederation, other kinds of tokens appeared, such as those for services, transportation and advertising purposes.

The prices in this section are for tokens in V.G. (Very Good) or F. (Fine) condition. Higher prices willl be paid for rare issues or for tokens in V.F. (Very Flne) or better condition.

NEWFOUNDLAND

Date and Description	Buying Price	Date and Description	Buying Price
Rutherford - St. John's	.75	1858 Sailing Ship	75.00
Rutherford - Harbour Grace	.75	1860 Fishery Rights	10.00
McAuslane	500.00		

Date and Description	Buying Price	Date and Description	Buying Price
Holey Dollar Ring	1,000.00	McCarthy Penny	500.00
Holey Dollar Plug	1,000.00	Sheaf of Wheat	100.00
McCausland Penny	500.00	Speed The Plough	.75

Note: Forgeries exist and are worth considerably less.

Date and Description	Buying Price	Date and Description	Buying Price
Fisheries & Agriculture	.75	Fisheries & Agriculture	.75

Self Government 1855
  Prince Edward's
	.75	Ships Colonies 1815
		  One Penny
			5.00

Self Government 1855
  Prince Edward
	.75	Ships Colonies 1815
		  Publick Accommodation
			5.00

Self Government 1857	.75	Ships Colonies	.75

NOVA SCOTIA

SEMI-REGAL TOKENS

Date and Description	Buying Price	Date and Description	Buying Price
1823 Halfpenny	.50	1840 Halfpenny	.50
1823 Penny	1.00	1840 Penny	1.00
1824 Halfpenny	.50	1843 Half Penny	.50
1824 Penny	1.00	1843 Penny	1.00
1832 Halfpenny	.50	1856 Halfpenny	.50
1832 Penny	1.00	1856 Penny	1.00

PRIVATE TOKENS

Date and Description	Buying Price	Date and Description	Buying Price
Broke - Halifax	2.00	Hosterman & Etter 1815	2.00
Convenience of Trade	3.00	Starr & Shannon	1.00
Carritt & Alport	3.00	Commercial Change	1.00
Hosterman & Etter	2.00	Miles W. White	1.00

Date and Description	Buying Price	Date and Description	Buying Price
John Alexr Barry	1.00	Trade & Navigation 1812	1.00
Halifax Nova Scotia	2.00	Trade & Navigation 1813	10.00
W. A. & S. Black's	2.00	Pure Copper Preferable	1.00
J. Brown	1.00	Success to Navigation	1.00
W. L. White's	10.00	N.S & N.B. Success	10.00

Date and Description	Buying Price	Date and Description	Buying Price
1843 Halfpenny	.50	McDermott	150.00
1843 Penny	.75	St. John	2.00
1854 Halfpenny	.50	St. John's	1,000.00
1854 Penny	.75		

LOWER CANADA

Date and Description	Buying Price	Date and Description	Buying Price
Magdalen Island	10.00	Pro Bono Publico	1,000.00
Bank Token	1.00	Bank Token Halfpenny	.75
Banque Du Peuple, Maple Leaf	1.00	Bank Token Penny	1.00
Banque Du Peuple, Wreath	1.00	Bank of Montreal	
		Sideview Halfpenny	200.00
		Sideview Penny	400.00

Date and Description	Buying Price	Date and Description	Buying Price
Montreal Half Penny	2.00	Francis Mullins & Son	3.00
Canada Half Penny	2.00	R.W. Owen	500.00
For Public Accommodation	2.00	J. Shaw & Co.	3.00
T.S. Brown & Co.	2.00	J. Roy	15.00
Ths & Wm Molson	75.00	Agriculture & Commerce	.75

Date and Description	Buying Price	Date and Description	Buying Price
Halfpenny Token 1812, Small Wreath	1.00	To Facilitate Trade	
Halfpenny Token 1812, Large Wreath	1.00	Military Bust 1825	2.00
Penny Token 1812	2.00	Civilian Bust 1825	500.00
Victoria Nobis Est	2.00	Spread Eagle	1.00
R H Half Penny	2.00	Halfpenny Token	2.00

Date and Description	Buying Price	Date and Description	Buying Price
Seated Justice	1.00	Commercial Change	2.00
Bust/Ships Colonies	1.00	Bust and Harp	1.00

WELLINGTON TOKENS

Date and Description	Buying Price	Date and Description	Buying Price
Field Marshal Wellington	1.00	The Illustrious Wellington	1.00
Marquis Wellington	2.00	Battle Token	1.00

Date and Description	Buying Price	Date and Description	Buying Price
Copper Company	100.00	Success To Commerce	1.00
Lesslie Halfpenny	2.00	Upper & Lower Canada	15.00
Lesslie Twopenny	20.00	Commercial Change 1815	10.00
No Labour No Bread	.75	Commerical Change 1820	1.00
Sir Isaac Brock	.75		

Date and Description	Buying Price	Date and Description	Buying Price
Commercial Change 1821		To Facilitate Trade	
Cask Marked Upper Canada	10.00	1823	2.00
Cask Marked Jamaica	200.00	1833	1.00
Upper Canada	5.00	Commercial Change 1833	2.00

PROVINCE OF CANADA TOKENS

Date and Description	Buying Price	Date and Description	Buying Price
Bank of Montreal 1837-1845		Quebec Bank 1852	
1842, 1844 Halfpenny	.50	Halfpenny	.50
1845 Halfpenny	1,000.00	Penny	1.00
1837 Penny	50.00	Bank of Upper Canada 1850-1857	
1842 Penny	1.00	Halfpenny	.50
		Penny	1.00

ANONYMOUS AND MISCELLANEOUS TOKENS

Date and Description	Buying Price	Date and Description	Buying Price
For General Accommodation	1.00	Pure Copper Preferable	1.00
Success to Trade	10.00	North American	10.00

72

BRITISH COLUMBIA

Date and Description	Buying Price
1802 Pattern Gold $10	Very Rare
1802 Pattern Gold $20	Very Rare

NORTH WEST COMPANY

Date and Description	Buying Price
1820 North West Company Token	100.00

HUDSON'S BAY COMPANY

Date and Description	Buying Price
Hudson's Bay Company Tokens Set of four (1, 1/2, 1/4, 1/8)	30.00

TRANSPORTATION TOKENS

Date and Description	Buying Price
Bridge Tokens, each	40.00
Montreal & Lachine Railroad	20.00

CANADIAN MEDALS

WAR MEDALS

Arny
Gold
Cross

Naval
General
Service
Medal

Army
Gold
Medal

Canadian
General
Service
Medal

Army
General
Service
Medal

Egyptian
Medal

Date and Description	Buying Price	Date and Description	Buying Price
Army Gold Cross	5,000.00	Canadian General Service Medal	
Army Gold Medal	2,000.00	Fenian Raid Bar 1866	75.00
Army General Service Medal 1812-1814		Fenian Raid Bar 1870	175.00
Fort Detroit Bar	525.00	Red River Bar 1870	200.00
Chateauguay Bar	525.00	Egyptian Medal*	
Chrysler's Farm Bar	750.00	The Nile Bar	400.00
Naval General Service Medal 1812-1814	200.00	Kirbekan Bar	400.00

*Awarded to Canadian Boatmen

Khedive's
Bronze
Star

1914
Star

North West
Canada
Medal

1914-1915
Star

South
Africa
Medal

British
War
Medal

Date and Description	Buying Price
Khedive's Bronze Star	15.00
North West Canada Medal 1885	100.00
Saskatchewan Bar	200.00
Queen's South Africa	
1899-1900 on reverse	1,000.00
Dates removed	15.00
King's South Africa	15.00

Date and Description	Buying Price
1914 Star*	500.00
1914-1915 Star	1.00
British War Medal	5.00

*Canadian Star awarded to 2nd. Field Hospital only.

Allied
Victory
Medal

Merchantile
Marine
War
Medal

WORLD WAR II

Canadian
Volunteer
Service
Medal

STARS

1939-1945
Atlantic
Air Crew
Europe
Africa
France and
Germanu
Italy
Pacific
Burma

The
Defence
Medal

WW II
1939-1945
War
Medal

Date and Description	Buying Price
Allied Victory Medal	1.00
Merchantile Marine War Medal	5.00
Canadian Volunteer Service Medal	8.00

Date and Description	Buying Price
1939-1945 Star	1.00
Atlantic Star	1.00
Air Crew Europe	30.00
Africa Star	1.00
France and Germany Star	1.00
Italy Star	1.00
Pacific Star	1.00
Burma Star	1.00
Defence Medal	8.00
1939-1945 War Medal	8.00

Canadian
Korean
Medal

Coronation
Medal - 1911

United
Nations
Korea
Medal

Silver
Jubilee
Medal - 1935

United
Nations
Emergency
Medal

Coronation
Medal - 1937

Date and Description	Buying Price	Date and Description	Buying Price
Canadian Korean War Medal, English	20.00	King George V	
Canadian Korean War Medal, French	30.00	Coronation Medal - 1911	7.00
United Nations Korea Medal	10.00	Silver Jubilee Medal - 1935	7.00
United Nations Emergency Medal	10.00	King George VI	
United Nations Medal 1960 to present	10.00	Coronation Medal - 1937	7.00
International Commission Medal 1967	10.00		
International Commission Medal 1973	10.00		

Coronation
Medal - 1953

Victoria
Cross

Silver
Jubilee
Medal - 1977

Distinguished
Service
Order

Canadian
Centennial
Medal - 1967

Date and Description	Buying Price
Queen Elizabeth II	
Coronation Medal - 1953	10.00
Silver Jubilee Medal - 1977	10.00
Canadian Centennial Medal - 1967	10.00

Order
of
Canada

Date and Description	Buying Price
Victoria Cross	10,000.00
Distinguished Service Order	250.00
Order of Canada: Officer	250.00
Member	500.00
Companion	2,500.00

Distinguished
Service
Cross

Distinguished
Flying
Cross

Air Force
Cross

Date and Description	Buying Price
Distinguished Service Cross	200.00
Distinguished Flying Cross	225.00
Air Force Cross	275.00

COINS OF THE UNITED STATES

MINT MARKS

The United States decimal coinage is identified by the following mint marks:

- C -Charlotte, North Carolina
- CC -Carson City, Nevada
- D -Dahlonega, George (gold coins only)
- D -Denver, Colorado (1906 to date)
- O -New Orleans, Louisiana
- S -San Francisco, California
- P -Philadelphia, Pennsylvania

HALF CENTS

Liberty Cap   **Classic Head**

Date and Mint Mark	Buying Price	Date and Mint Mark	Buying Price
1793	500.00	1809-1810	7.00
1794	150.00	1811	30.00
1795	100.00	1825 to 1835	7.00
1796	1,000.00		
1797	100.00		

Braided Hair

Draped Bust

Date and Mint Mark	Buying Price
1849 to 1857	7.00

Date and Mint Mark	Buying Price
1800	10.00
1802	150.00
1803-1808	8.00

IMPORTANT

Do not clean your coins. Coins should be handled carefully. Only experts should consider cleaning. If you are not an expert the results can be disastrous.

LARGE CENTS

Flowing Hair

Date and Mint Mark	Buying Price
1793	500.00

Liberty Cap

Date and Mint Mark	Buying Price
1793	300.00
1794	30.00
1795	25.00
1796	30.00

Draped Bust

Date and Mint Mark	Buying Price
1796	20.00
1797	10.00
1798	5.00
1799	200.00
1800 to 1803	5.00
1804	125.00
1805 to 1807	4.00

Classic Head

Date and Mint Mark	Buying Price
1808	8.00
1809	30.00
1810	6.00
1811	15.00
1812 to 1814	6.00

Coronet Head

Date and Mint Mark	Buying Price
1816 to 1820	2.00
1821	4.00
1822	2.00
1823	8.00
1824 to 1838	2.00
1839 to 1856	1.00
1857	4.00

SMALL CENTS

Flying Eagle

Date and Mint Mark	Buying Price
1856	500.00
1857 to 1858	2.00

Indian Head

Date and Mint Mark	Buying Price
1859 to 1865	.50
1866 to 1868	3.00
1869 to 1872	4.00
1873 to 1876	1.00
1877	50.00
1878 to 1886	.20
1887 to 1908	.10
1908S	4.00
1909	.10
1909S	25.00

Lincoln Head Wheat Ears

Date and Mint Mark	Buying Price
1909	.03
1909VDB	.10
1909S	5.00
1909SVDB	40.00
1910 to 1914	.03
1914D	10.00
1915D to 1931D	.02
1931S	5.00
1932 to 1954	.01

Lincoln Head Memorial

Date and Mint Mark	Buying Price
1955 Double Date	20.00
1955 to 1992	.01

TWO CENTS

Date and Mint Mark	Buying Price
1864 to 1871	1.50
1872	10.00
1873 Proof	500.00

THREE CENTS

Silver

Date and Mint Mark	Buying Price
1851 to 1862	2.00
1863 to 1873 Proof	300.00

Nickel

Date and Mint Mark	Buying Price
1865 to 1874	.75
1875 to 1876	1.00
1877 to 1878 Proof	250.00
1879 to 1880	15.00
1881	.75
1882	10.00
1883	20.00
1884 to 1887	15.00
1888 to 1889	10.00

FIVE CENTS NICKEL

Shield

Date and Mint Mark	Buying Price
1866 to 1876	1.50
1879 to 1881	17.00
1882 to 1883	1.50

Liberty Head

Date and Mint Mark	Buying Price
1883 to 1884	.30
1885	60.00
1886	15.00
1887 to 1912	.10
1912S	7.00

Indian Head or Buffalo Type

Date and Mint Mark	Buying Price
1913	.10
1914 to 1918	.10
1918D 8/7	100.00
1919 to 1938	.10

Jefferson Type

Date and Mint Mark	Buying Price
1938 to 1992	.05

HALF DIMES

Flowing Hair

Date and Mint Mark	Buying Price
1794	200.00
1795	125.00

Draped Bust

Date and Mint Mark	Buying Price
1796 to 1797	225.00
1800 to 1801	200.00
1802	2,000.00
1803 to 1805	200.00

Capped Bust

Date and Mint Mark	Buying Price
1829 to 1837	3.00

Liberty Seated

Date and Mint Mark	Buying Price
1837	6.00
1838 No Stars	12.00
1838 to 1845	1.00
1846	35.00
1847 to 1863	1.00
1864	20.00
1864S	1.00
1865	30.00
1866	17.00
1866S	1.00
1867	20.00
1867S	1.00
1868 to 1873	.75

DIMES

Draped Bust

Date and Mint Mark	Buying Price
1796 to 1979	300.00
1798 to 1807	150.00

Capped Bust

Date and Mint Mark	Buying Price
1809 to 1811	10.00
1814 to 1821	6.00
1822	15.00
1823 to 1837	5.00

Liberty Seated

Date and Mint Mark	Buying Price
1837 to 1838	7.00
1839 to 1843	1.00
1844	10.00
1845	.75
1846	15.00
1847 to 1856	1.00
1856S	10.00
1857 to 1860	1.00
1858S	10.00
1859S	10.00
1860O	65.00
1861 to 1862	.75
1863	20.00
1864 to 1867	25.00
1864S to 1867S	2.00
1868 to 1874	1.00
1871CC	100.00
1872CC	60.00
1873CC	125.00
1874CC	150.00
1875 to 1878	1.00
1878CC	3.00
1879	17.00
1880 to 1881	15.00
1882 to 1885	1.00
1885S	17.00
1886 to 1891	1.00

Barber

Date and Mint Mark	Buying Price
1892 to 1895	.60
1895oO	20.00
1896O	10.00
1897 to 1916	.20

Mercury Head

Date and Mint Mark	Buying Price
1916	.20
1916D	100.00
1917 to 1945	.20

Roosevelt - Silver

Date and Mint Mark	Buying Price
1946 to 1964	.20

Roosevelt - Clad

Date and Mint Mark	Buying Price
1965 to 1992	.10

TWENTY CENTS

Date and Mint Mark	Buying Price
1875 to 1876	15.00
1877 to 1878 Proof	1,000.00

QUARTER DOLLAR

Draped Bust

Date and Mint Mark	Buying Price
1796	1,000.00
1804	100.00
1805 to 1807	60.00

Capped Bust

Date and Mint Mark	Buying Price
1815 to 1822	12.00
1823	1,000.00
1824 to 1838	12.00

Liberty Seated

Date and Mint Mark	Buying Price
1838 to 1849	3.00
1849O	60.00
1850 to 1851	4.00
1851O	20.00
1852	4.00
1852O	20.00

Date and Mint Mark	Buying Price
1853 No Arrows	25.00
1853 to 1873	1.50
1870CC	150.00
1871CC	100.00
1871S	5.00
1872CC	70.00
1874 to 1878	1.50
1879 to 1888	20.00
1889 to 1891	1.40

Washington - Silver

Date and Mint Mark	Buying Price
1932 to 1964	.50

Washington - Clad

Date and Mint Mark	Buying Price
1965 to 1975	.25

Barber

Date and Mint Mark	Buying Price
1892 to 1896	1.00
1896S	75.00
1897 to 1901	1.00
1901S	300.00
1902 to 1913	1.00
1913S	75.00
1914 to 1916	1.00

200th Bi-Centennial

Date and Mint Mark	Buying Price
1976	.25

Standing Liberty

Date and Mint Mark	Buying Price
1916	300.00
1917 to 1930	.50

Washington - Clad

Date and Mint Mark	Buying Price
1977 to 1992	.25

HALF DOLLARS

Flowing Hair

Date and Mint Mark	Buying Price
1794	300.00
1795	175.00

Draped Bust

Date and Mint Mark	Buying Price
1796 15 Stars	2,400.00
1796 16 Stars	2,400.00
1797 15 Stars	2,400.00
1801 to 1802	45.00
1803 to 1807	25.00

Capped Bust

Date and Mint Mark	Buying Price
1807	15.00
1808 to 1814	7.00

Date and Mint Mark	Buying Price
1815	175.00
1817 to 1836	5.00
1836 Reeded Edge	100.00
1837 to 1839'	10.00
1839O	25.00

Liberty Seated

Date and Mint Mark	Buying Price
1839 to 1852	4.00
1850	10.00
1851	10.00
1852	20.00
1852O	10.00
1853 to 1855	3.00
1855S Arrows	25.00
1856 to 1878	3.00
1870CC	100.00
1871CC to 1878CC	10.00
1878S	800.00
1879 to 1890	50.00
1891	3.00

Barber

Date and Mint Mark	Buying Price
1892	3.00
1892O and 1892S	20.00
1893 to 1897	2.50
1870O	10.00
1897S	10.00
1898 to 1915	1.50

Liberty Walking

Date and Mint Mark	Buying Price
1916 to 1920	1.00
1921	15.00
1921D	20.00
1923 to 1947	1.00

Franklin

Date and Mint Mark	Buying Price
1948 to 1963	1.00

Kennedy - Silver

Date and Mint Mark	Buying Price
1964	1.00

Kennedy - Silver Clad

Date and Mint Mark	Buying Price
1965 to 1970	.55

Kennedy - Copper Clad

Date and Mint Mark	Buying Price
1971 to 1992	.50

SILVER DOLLARS

Flowing Hair

Date and Mint Mark	Buying Price
1794	2,000.00
1795	300.00

Draped Bust

Date and Mint Mark	Buying Price
1795	300.00
1796 to 1798	250.00
1798 to 1803	125.00

Liberty Seated

Date and Mint Mark	Buying Price
1840 to 1873	25.00
1870CC	7,500.00
1871CC	175.00
1872CC	175.00
1872S	40.00
1873CC	500.00

Liberty Head

Date and Mint Mark	Buying Price
1878 to 1892	5.00
1879CC and 1881CC	20.00
1882CC and 1884CC	10.00
1885CC	40.00
1889CC	80.00
1893CC	30.00
1893O	25.00
1893S	400.00
1894	100.00
1895O	25.00
1895S	40.00
1896 to 1903	5.00
1903O	40.00
1904 to 1921	5.00

Peace

Date and Mint Mark	Buying Price
1921 to 1927	5.00
1928	30.00
1928S to 1935	5.00

Eisenhower

Date and Mint Mark	Buying Price
1971 to 1976	1.00

Susan B. Anthony

Date and Mint Mark	Buying Price
1979 to 1981	1.00

TRADE DOLLARS

Date and Mint Mark	Buying Price
1873 to 1878	20.00
1878CC	40.00

GOLD COINS

DOLLARS

Type 1 Liberty Head

Date and Mint Mark	Buying Price
1849 to 1854	60.00

Type 2 Indian Head Small

Date and Mint Mark	Buying Price
1854 to 1855	100.00
1855C	300.00
1855D	700.00

Type 3 Indian Head Large

Date and Mint Mark	Buying Price
1855 to 1889	75.00
1855D	700.00
1856D	1,400.00
1860D	1,100.00
1861D	2,000.00
1875	900.00

QUARTER EAGLES (2 1/2 DOLLARS)

Capped Bust Right

Date and Mint Mark	Buying Price
1796	3,700.00
1797 to 1807	1,300.00

Capped Bust Left

Date and Mint Mark	Buying Price
1808	3,500.00

Capped Head Left

Date and Mint Mark	Buying Price
1821 to 1827	1,500.00
1829 to 1833	1,400.00
1834	3,500.00

Classic Head

Date and Mint Mark	Buying Price
1834 to 1839	100.00

Coronet Head

Date and Mint Mark	Buying Price
1840 to 1907	70.00
1843S/D Cr 4	325.00
1848 California	3,000.00
1854D	500.00
1854S	5,000.00
1855D	600.00
1856D	1,700.00
1875	2,000.00

Indian Head

Date and Mint Mark	Buying Price
1908 to 1929	65.00
1911D	250.00

3 DOLLARS

Date and Mint Mark	Buying Price
1854 to 1873	220.00
1854D	2,500.00
1873 Closed 3	1,250.00
1880 to 1889	240.00

4 DOLLARS

Date and Mint Mark	Buying Price
1879 to 1880 Proof	15,000.00

HALF EAGLES
(5 DOLLARS)

Capped Bust Right

Date and Mint Mark	Buying Price
1795 to 1797	2,600.00
1798 to 1807	500.00

Draped Bust Left

Date and Mint Mark	Buying Price
1807 to 1834	500.00
1821	1,000.00
1822	125,000.00
1823	800.00
1824	2,000.00
1825	17,500.00
1826	1,400.00
1827	2,500.00
1828	2,500.00
1829	10,000.00

Classic Head

Date and Mint Mark	Buying Price
1834 to 1838	100.00
1838C	250.00
1838D	200.00

Coronet Head

Date and Mint Mark	Buying Price
1839 to 1908	70.00
1842C Small Date	800.00
1854S	5,000.00
1861C	300.00
1861D	1,400.00
1862S	700.00
1864S	1,100.00
1870CC	600.00
1875	3,000.00
1878CC	500.00

Indian Head

Date and Mint Mark	Buying Price
1908 to 1916	850.00
1929	1,800.00

EAGLE
(10 DOLLARS)

Capped Bust Right

Date and Mint Mark	Buying Price
Small Eagle, 1795 to 1797	2,800.00
Heraldic Eagle, 1797 to 1803	1,000.00

Coronet Head

Date and Mint Mark	Buying Price
1838 to 1907	180.00
1858	2,500.00
1859O	600.00
1859S	500.00
1863	1,800.00
1864S	750.00
1865S	750.00
1866S	300.00
1870CC	700.00
1873	2,000.00
1873CC	350.00
1875 Proof	8,000.00
1876	1,400.00
1877	1,100.00
1877CC	350.00
1878CC	600.00
1879CC	1,250.00
1879O	900.00
1883O	500.00

$10 Indian Head

Date and Mint Mark	Buying Price
1907 to 1932	190.00
1920S	2,000.00
1930S	3,500.00
1933	10,000.00

DOUBLE EAGLES ($20 DOLLARS)

Liberty

Date and Mint Mark	Buying Price
1849 to 1907	350.00
1854O	7,000.00
1855O	800.00
1856O	7,000.00
1859O	800.00
1860O	1,200.00
1861O	800.00
1870CC	7,000.00
1871CC	600.00
1879O	1,000.00
1881	1,100.00
1882	3,000.00
1885	3,600.00
1886	2,900.00
1891	1,600.00
1891CC	500.00

$20 St. Gaudens

Date and Mint Mark	Buying Price
1907 MCMVII	1,300.00
1907 to 1916	400.00
1920S	3,000.00
1921	3,500.00
1922 to 1928	400.00
1927D	100,000.00
1927S	2,300.00
1929	2,300.00
1930 to 1932	4,000.00

US Gold coins must be in VF or better condition, badly worn or damaged coins will be discounted from these prices.

GOLD COMMEMORATIVE COINS

Date and Mint Mark	Buying Price
1903 $1 Louisiana Purchase, Jefferson	90.00
1903 $1 Louisiana Purchase, McKinley	90.00
1904 $1 Louis & Clark Exposition	115.00
1905 $1 Louis & Clark Exposition	115.00
1915S $1 Panama-Pacific Exposition	90.00
1916 $1 McKinley Memorial	90.00
1917 $1 McKinley Memorial	90.00
1922 $1 Grant Memorial, With Star	300.00
1922 $1 Grant Memorial, Without Star	300.00
1915S $2.50 Panama-Pacific Exposition	250.00
1926 $2.50 Philadelphia Sesquicentennial	150.00
1984P $10 Olympic	200.00
1984D $10 Olympic	200.00
1984S $10 Olympic	200.00
1984W $10 Olympic	200.00
1986W $5 Liberty	80.00
1987W $5 Constitution	80.00
1988W $5 Oylmpic	80.00
1989W $5 Congress	80.00

WORLD GOLD COINS

This partial listing of world gold coins indicates the prices dealers are willing to pay based on the Canadian dollar gold price as at May 10, 1991. Prices will fluctuate with the market price of gold plus the Canadian/U.S. dollar exchange rate.

AUSTRIA

Date and Denom.	Fine Gold Content oz	Buying Price
1912 10K	0.0980	32.75
1915 20K	0.1960	65.50
1915 100K	0.9803	327.00
1915 1D	0.1109	37.00
1914 4D	0.4438	148.00
1892 10Fr	0.0933	31.00
1892 20Fr*	0.1867	62.00

BAHAMAS

Date and Denom.	Fine Gold Content oz	Buying Price
1967 $10	0.1177	39.25
1971 $10	0.1177	39.25
1972 $10	0.0940	31.25
1967 $20	0.2355	78.50
1971 $20*	0.2355	78.50
1972 $20	0.1880	62.75
1967 $50	0.5888	196.50
1971 $50	0.5888	196.50
1972 $50	0.4708	157.00
1967 $100	1.1776	393.00
1971 $100	1.1776	393.00
1972 $100	0.9420	314.25

BELGIUM

Date and Denom.	Fine Gold Content oz	Buying Price
1867 to 1914 20Fr	0.1867	62.30

BERMUDA

Date and Denom.	Fine Gold Content oz	Buying Price
1970 $20	0.2355	78.50
1977 $50	0.1172	39.00
1975 $100*	0.2304	77.00
1977 $100	0.2344	78.25

CAYMAN ISLANDS

Date and Denom.	Fine Gold Content oz	Buying Price
1972 $25*	0.2532	84.50
1974 $50	0.1823	61.00
1974 $100	0.3646	121.50
1975 $100	0.3646	121.50
1977 $100	0.3464	115.50

* Coin illustrated

CHILE

Date and Denom.	Fine Gold Content oz	Buying Price
1898 to 1900 5p	0.0883	29.50
1896 to 1901 10p*	0.1766	59.00
1896 to 1917 20p	0.3532	118.00
1926 to 1980 100p	0.5886	196.50

COLUMBIA

Date and Denom.	Fine Gold Content oz	Buying Price
1913 to 1929 2 1/2p	0.1177	39.25
1913 to 1930 5p	0.2355	78.50
1919 and 1924 10p	0.4710	157.00
1973 1500p*	0.5527	184.50

FRANCE

Date and Denom.	Fine Gold Content oz	Buying Price
1856 to 1869 5Fr	0.0467	15.50
1854 to 1914 10Fr	0.0933	31.00
1809 to 1914 20Fr*	0.1867	62.00
1810 to 1838 40Fr	0.3734	124.00
1855 to 1864 50Fr	0.4667	155.75
1855 to 1913 100Fr	0.9335	311.50

GERMANY

Date and Denom.	Fine Gold Content oz	Buying Price
1872 to 1914 10DM	0.1152	38.50
1871 to 1914 20DM*	0.2304	77.00

GREAT BRITAIN

Date and Denom.	Fine Gold Content oz	Buying Price
1863 to 1915 1/2 Sov.	0.1177	39.25
1871 to 1968 Sov.*	0.2354	78.50
1887 Two Pound	0.4708	157.00
1897 Two Pound	0.4708	157.00
1902 Two Pound	0.4708	157.00
1911 Two Pound	0.4708	157.00
1937 Two Pound	0.4708	157.00
1887 Five Pound	1.1773	392.50
1897 Five Pound	1.1773	392.50
1902 Five Pound	1.1773	392.50
1911 Five Pound	1.1773	392.50
1937 Five Pound	1.1773	392.50

IRAN

Date and Denom.	Fine Gold Content oz	Buying Price
1971 500R	0.1883	63.00
1971 750R*	0.2827	94.25
1971 1000R	0.3770	126.00
1971 2000R	0.7541	251.50

ITALY

Date and Denom.	Fine Gold Content oz	Buying Price
1932 to 1860 10L	0.0931	31.00
1831 to 1860 20L*	0.1866	62.25
1822 to 1831 40L	0.3733	124.50
1832 to 1844 100L	0.9332	311.50

NETHERLANDS

Date and Denom.	Fine Gold Content oz	Buying Price
1900 to 1937 1D*	0.1109	37.00
1912 5G	0.0973	32.50
1875 to 1933 10G	0.1947	65.00

JAMAICA

Date and Denom.	Fine Gold Content oz	Buying Price
1972 $20*	0.2531	84.50
1975, 1976 $100	0.2265	75.50
1978 $100	0.3281	109.50
1978, 1979 $250	1.2507	417.50

PANAMA

Date and Denom.	Fine Gold Content oz	Buying Price
1975 to 1979 100B*	0.2361	78.75
1975 to 1979 500B	1.2067	402.50

MEXICO

Date and Denom.	Fine Gold Content oz	Buying Price
1945 2p	0.0482	16.00
1945 2 1/2p	0.0602	20.00
1955 5p	0.1205	40.00
1959 10p*	0.2411	80.50
1959 20p	0.4823	161.00
1947 50p	1.2057	402.50

Above dates are restrikes.

RUSSIA

Date and Denom.	Fine Gold Content oz	Buying Price
1897 to 1911 5R*	0.1244	41.50
1897 7 1/2R	0.1867	62.25
1898 to 1911 10R	0.2489	83.00
1897 15R	0.3734	124.50
1977 to 1988 100R	0.5000	167.00

IMPORTANT
Buying prices are listed for coins graded VF
or better. Bent, damaged or badly worn
coins are worth less.

*Coin illustrated.

APPENDIX - BULLION VALUES

Silver and gold coins and other numismatic items are often bought by dealers for their bullion value, that is the value of the pure precious metals which they contain. The weight of precious metals is expressed in grams or troy ounces, not in avoirdupois ounces. A troy ounce is greater than an avoirdupois ounce.

1 Troy Ounce = 31.103 Grams / 1 Avoirdupois Ounce = 28.349 Grams

GOLD

The quantity of pure gold in gold coins is calculated by multiplying the gold fineness or purity of the coin by its weight in troy ounces or grams. Gold purity can also be expressed in karats, a 24-part system with 24-karats equalling pure gold, 22 karats equalling 22 parts gold to 2 parts base metal, 18 karats equalling 18 part gold to 6 parts base metal etc.

A 14-karat or .585 fine gold coin weighing 1 troy ounce contains 1 ounce x .585 = .585 troy ounces of pure gold. If gold is worth $600 per troy ounce, then this coin is worth $600 x .585 = $351. (See extended charts.)

SILVER

The quantity of pure silver in silver coins is calculated by multiplying the silver fineness or purity of the coin by its weight in troy ounces.

A .800 fine silver coin weighing 1 troy ounce contains 1 x .800 = .800 troy ounces or pure silver. If silver is worth $20 and ounce, then this coin is worth $20 x .800 = $16. (See extended charts.)

GOLD CONTENT OF CANADIAN GOLD COINS

Denom.	Date and Mint Mark	Gross Weight (Grams)	Fineness	Pure Gold Content Grams	Troy Oz.
NEWFOUNDLAND					
$2	1865-1888	3.33	.917	3.05	.100
CANADA					
1 pd.	1908C-1910C	7.99	.917	7.32	.236
1 pd.	1911C-1919C	7.99	.917	7.32	.236
$5	1912-1914	8.36	.900	7.52	.242
$10	1912-1914	16.72	.900	15.05	.484
$20	1967	18.27	.900	16.45	.529
$5 M.L.	1982 to Date	3.11	.9999	3.11	.10
$10 M.L.	1982 to Date	7.78	.9999	7.78	.25
$20 M.L.	1986 to Date	15.57	.9999	15.57	.500
$50 M.L.	1979 to Date	31.10	.999	31.10	1.000
$100	1976 (Unc.)	13.33	.583	7.78	.250
$100	1976 (Proof)	16.96	.917	15.55	.499
$100	1977-1986	16.96	.917	15.55	.499
$100	1987 to Date	13.33	.583	7.78	.250

SILVER CONTENT OF CANADIAN SILVER COINS

Denom.	Date	Fineness	Silver Content Grams	Troy Oz.
$20	1985-1988	.925	31.103	1.000
$10	1973-1976	.925	44.955	1.445
$5	1973-1976	.925	22.477	.723
$5 M.L.	1987 to Date	.999	31.103	1.000
$1	1935-1967	.800	18.661	.600
$1	1971 to Date	.500	11.662	.375
50-cents	1870-1919	.925	10.792	.347
50-cents	1920-1967	.800	9.330	.300
25-cents	1870-1919	.925	5.370	.173
25-cents	1920-1967	.800	4.665	.150
25-cents	1967-1968	.500	2.923	.094
10-cents	1858-1919	.925	2.146	.069
10-cents	1920-1967	.800	1.866	.060
10-cents	1967-1968	.500	1.170	.038
5-cents	1858-1919	.925	1.080	.034
5-cents	1920-1921	.800	.933	.030

BULLION VALUES OF CANADIAN GOLD COINS
Computed from $300 to $700 per troy ounce in increments of $100 Canadian.

Denomination	Date and Mint Mark	$300	$400	$500	$600	$700
NEWFOUNDLAND						
$2	1865-1888	30.00	40.00	50.00	60.00	70.00
CANADA						
1 pd.	1908C-1910C	70.95	94.40	118.00	141.60	165.20
1 pd.	1911C-1919C	70.95	94.40	118.00	141.60	165.20
$5	1912-1914	72.60	96.80	121.00	145.20	160.40
$10	1912-1914	145.20	193.60	242.00	290.40	338.00
$20	1967	158.70	211.60	264.50	317.40	370.30
$5 M.L.	1982 to Date	30.00	40.00	50.00	60.00	70.00
$10 M.L.	1982 to Date	75.00	100.00	125.00	150.00	175.00
$20 M.L.	1986 to Date	150.00	200.00	250.00	300.00	350.00
$50 M.L.	1979 to Date	300.00	400.00	500.00	600.00	700.00
$100	1976 (Unc.)	75.00	100.00	125.00	150.00	175.00
$100	1976 (Pf)	150.00	200.00	250.00	300.00	350.00
$100	1977-1986	150.00	200.00	250.00	300.00	350.00
$100	1987 (Pf)	75.00	100.00	125.00	150.00	175.00

BULLION VALUES OF CANADIAN SILVER COINS
Computed from $5 to $50 per troy ounce in increments of $10 Canadian.

Denom.	Fineness	$5	$10	$20	$30	$40	$50
$20	.925	5.00	10.00	20.00	30.00	40.00	50.00
$10	.925	7.23	14.00	28.90	43.35	57.80	72.15
$5	.925	3.62	7.23	14.46	21.69	28.92	36.15
$5 M.L.	.999	5.00	10.00	20.00	30.00	40.00	50.00
$1	.800	3.00	6.00	12.00	18.00	24.00	30.00
$1	.500	1.88	3.75	7.50	11.25	15.00	18.75
50-cents	.925	1.74	3.47	6.94	10.41	13.88	17.35
50-cents	.800	1.50	3.00	6.00	9.00	12.00	15.00
25-cents	.925	.87	1.73	3.46	5.19	6.92	8.65
25-cents	.800	.75	1.50	3.00	4.50	6.00	7.50
25-cents	.500	.47	.94	1.88	2.82	3.76	4.70
10-cents	.925	.35	.69	1.38	2.07	2.76	3.45
10-cents	.800	.30	.60	1.20	1.80	2.40	3.00
10-cents	.500	.19	.38	.76	1.14	1.52	1.90
5-cents	.925	.17	.34	.68	1.02	1.36	1.70
5-cents	.800	.15	.30	.60	.90	1.20	1.50